Congressional
Research
Service

House Committee on Ethics: A Brief History of Its Evolution and Jurisdiction

Jacob R. Straus
Analyst on the Congress

November 27, 2013

Congressional Research Service

7-5700

www.crs.gov

98-15

CRS Report for Congress

Prepared for Members and Committees of Congress

Summary

The *United States Constitution* (Article 1, Section 5, clause 1) provides each House of Congress with the sole authority to establish rules, judge membership requirements, and punish and expel Members. From 1789 to 1967, the House of Representatives dealt with disciplinary action against Members on a case-by-case basis, often forming ad-hoc committees to investigate and make recommendations when acts of wrongdoing were brought to the chamber's attention. Events of the 1960's, including the investigation of Representative Adam Clayton Powell for alleged misuse of Education and Labor Committee funds, prompted the creation of a permanent ethics committee and the writing of a Code of Conduct for Members, officers, and staff of the House.

Begun as a select committee in the 89th Congress (1965-1966), the House created a 12-member panel to "recommend to the House ... such ... rules or regulations ... necessary or desirable to insure proper standards of conduct by Members of the House and by officers and employees of the House, in the performance of their duties and the discharge of their responsibilities." Acting on the select committee's recommendations, the House created a permanent Committee on Standards of Official Conduct in the 90th Congress (1967-1968). In the 112th Congress (2011-2012), the committee was renamed the Committee on Ethics.

This report briefly outlines the background of ethics enforcement in the House of Representatives, including the creation of both the Select Committee on Ethics and the Committee on Ethics. The report also focuses on various jurisdictional and procedural changes that the committee has experienced since 1967 and discusses the committee's current jurisdiction and procedures.

For additional information on ethics in the House of Representatives, please refer to CRS Report R40760, *House Office of Congressional Ethics: History, Authority, and Procedures*, by Jacob R. Straus; CRS Report RL30764, *Enforcement of Congressional Rules of Conduct: An Historical Overview*, by Jacob R. Straus; CRS Report RL31126, *Lobbying Congress: An Overview of Legal Provisions and Congressional Ethics Rules*, by Jack Maskell; CRS Report RL31382, *Expulsion, Censure, Reprimand, and Fine: Legislative Discipline in the House of Representatives*, by Jack Maskell; and CRS Report R42495, *The STOCK Act, Insider Trading, and Public Financial Reporting by Federal Officials*, by Jack Maskell.

Contents

Tables

Appendixes

Contacts

Introduction

In the *Federalist Papers*, James Madison noted the importance of participation by upstanding citizens at all levels of government as a condition for legitimate governance. "The aim of every political constitution is, or ought to be, first to obtain for rulers men who possess most wisdom to discern, and most virtue to pursue, the common good of the society; and in the next place, to take the most effectual precautions for keeping them virtuous whilst they continue to hold their public trust."[1]

To ensure that Members uphold high standards, the Constitution provides each House of Congress sole authority to establish rules, judge membership requirements, and punish and expel its Members. Article I, Section 5, clause 1 provides that "Each House shall be the Judge of the Elections, Returns, and Qualifications of its own Members."[2] In addition, clause 2 provides that "Each House may determine the Rules of its Proceedings, punish its Members for disorderly Behaviour, and, with the Concurrence of two thirds, expel a Member."[3] Congress used their ability to establish ethics rules and to punish individual Members sparingly in the 18th and 19th centuries.[4]

As former Senate historian Richard Baker observed on the subject of congressional ethics, "[f]or nearly two centuries, a simple and informal code of behavior existed. Prevailing norms of general decency served as the chief determinants of proper legislative conduct."[5] During that time, Congress often dealt with potential ethics issues "on a case-by-case basis, only with the most obvious acts of wrongdoing, those clearly 'inconsistent with the trust and duty of a member.'"[6] Events in the 1960s, including the investigation of Representative Adam Clayton Powell's alleged misuse of Education and Labor Committee funds,[7] prompted a special subcommittee of the Committee on House Administration to investigate the allegations and the potential creation of an ethics committee to establish a code of conduct for the House of Representatives.[8]

This report examines the history and evolution of the House Committee on Ethics, including the committee's jurisdiction and investigative procedure. It does not deal with changes to federal or

---

[1] James Madison, "Federalist No. 57, The Alleged Tendency of the New Plan to Elevate the Few at the Expense of the Many Considered in Connection with Representation," *The Federalist Papers*, February 19, 1788, from the *New York Packet*, http://thomas.loc.gov/home/histdox/fed_57 html.

[2] U.S. Congress, "Article I, Section 5, clause 2," *The Constitution of the United States*, 108th Cong., 1st sess., H.Doc. 108-96 (Washington: GPO, 2003), p. 4.

[3] Ibid.

[4] U.S. Congress, Committee on House Administration, *History of the United States House of Representatives, 1789-1994*, 103rd Cong., 2nd sess., H.Doc. 103-324 (Washington: GPO, 1994), p. 293.

[5] Richard Baker, "The History of Congressional Ethics," in Bruce Jennings and Daniel Callahan, eds., *Representation and Responsibility: Exploring Legislative Ethics* (New York: Plenum Press, 1985), p. 4. [Hereafter, Baker, "The History of Congressional Ethics"].

[6] Baker, "The History of Congressional Ethics," p. 3.

[7] U.S. Congress, House, Select Committee Pursuant to House Resolution 1, *In Re Adam Clayton Powell*, report to accompany H.Res. 278, 90th Cong., 1st sess., February 23, 1967, H.Rept. 90-27 (Washington: GPO, 1967); and *Powell v. McCormick*, 395 U.S. 486 (1969).

[8] Robert V. Remini, *The House: The History of the House of Representatives* (Washington: Smithsonian Books, 2006), p. 414.

---

state criminal law or with criminal prosecutions of Members of Congress or with the specifics of disciplinary cases in the House.[9]

Creating a Permanent Ethics Committee

Prior to the creation of the House Committee on Standards of Official Conduct in the 90th Congress (1967-1968), no uniform mechanism existed for self-discipline in the House of Representatives. Congress, however, had previously attempted to create an ethical framework for House Members and employees. In 1958, Congress established the first Code of Ethics for Government Service.[10] Initially proposed in 1951 by Representative Charles Bennett, the Code of Ethics was adopted as a result of a House investigation of presidential chief of staff Sherman Adams, who was alleged to have received gifts from an industrialist being investigated by the Federal Trade Commission.[11] The Code of Ethics for Government Service standards continue to be recognized as ethical guidance in the House and Senate. They are, however, not legally binding because the code was adopted by congressional resolution, not by law.[12]

In the period preceding the creation of the Committee on Standards of Official Conduct in 1967, investigations into alleged wrongdoing by Members and staff of the House were dealt with in an ad-hoc fashion.[13] There were, however, attempts to create a more uniform system to investigate and discipline Members and staff.[14] For example, during hearings before the Joint Committee on the Organization of Congress in 1965, considerable testimony was presented on the ethical conduct of Members, and the need for House and Senate codes of conduct, financial disclosure regulations, and a House Ethics Committee (the Senate had created one in 1964).[15] In its final report, the Joint Committee called for the creation of a Committee on Standards and Conduct in the House.[16]

---

[9] For more information on Members indicted or convicted of a felony, see CRS Report RL33229, *Status of a Member of the House Who Has Been Indicted for or Convicted of a Felony*, by Jack Maskell. For more information on the enforcement of codes of Conduct in the House of Representatives and the Senate, see CRS Report RL30764, *Enforcement of Congressional Rules of Conduct: An Historical Overview*, by Jacob R. Straus.

[10] 72 Stat. B12, H.Con.Res. 175, July 11, 1958. See also "Code of Ethics For Government Service," House proceeding, *Congressional Record*, vol. 103, part 12 (August 28, 1957), p. 16297; and "Code of Ethics For Government Service," Senate proceeding, *Congressional Record*, vol. 104, part 10 (July 11, 1958), p. 13556.

[11] Rep. Charles Bennett, "Code of Ethics for Government Service," remarks in the House, *Congressional Record*, vol. 97, part 5 (June 26, 1951), pp. 7176-7178; and Testimony of Rep. Charles Bennett, in U.S. Congress, House Committee on Post Office and Civil Service, *Code of Ethics For Government Service*, hearings, 84th Cong., 2nd sess., March 29, 1956 (Washington: GPO, 1956), pp. 3-5.

[12] Because the code was adopted by concurrent resolution rather than statute, it does not have the force of law and technically expired at the end of the Congress adopting it. The Code of Ethics for Government Service is, however, cited by many House and Senate investigations. For example, see U.S. Congress, House, Committee on Standards of Official Conduct, *Investigation of Certain Allegations Related to Voting on the Medicare Prescription Drug, Improvement, and Modernization Act of 2003*, report, 108th Cong., 2nd sess., H.Rept. 108-722 (Washington: GPO, 2004), p. 38; and U. S. Congress, Senate Select Committee on Ethics, *Korean Influence Investigation*, report, 95th Cong., 2nd sess., S. Rept. 95-1314 (Washington: GPO, 1975), pp. 5-6.

[13] Baker, "The History of Congressional Ethics," p. 4.

[14] "Ethics," in *Congress and the Nation, 1945-1964* (Washington: Congressional Quarterly Inc., 1965), p. 1409.

[15] U.S. Congress, Joint Committee on the Organization of Congress, *Index to Hearings Before the Joint Committee on the Organization of Congress*, pursuant to S.Res. 2, 89th Cong, 1st and 2nd sess., various dates 1965 and 1966, part 16 (Washington: GPO, 1966), p. 45.

[16] U.S. Congress, Joint Committee on the Organization of Congress, *Organization of Congress*, final report pursuant to (continued...)

Select Committee on Standards and Conduct

On September 2, 1966, following publicized allegations of misconduct by House Education and Labor Committee Chair Adam Clayton Powell, Representative Charles Bennett introduced H.Res. 1013 to create a Select Committee on Standards and Conduct, which was referred to the Committee on Rules.[17] On September 7, the Committee on Rules reported the resolution "with the recommendation that the resolution do pass."[18] On October 19, the House debated, amended, and agreed to H.Res. 1013, creating the select committee.[19]

As adopted, the resolution created a 12-member panel, with six majority and six minority Members appointed by the Speaker of the House. The Select Committee was charged with two duties. They were to

> (1) recommend to the House, by report or resolution such additional rules or regulations as the Select Committee shall determine to be necessary or desirable to insure proper standards of conduct by Members of the House and by officers or employees of the House, in the performance of their duties and the discharge of their responsibilities; and

> (2) report violations, by a majority vote of the Select Committee, of any law to the proper Federal and State authorities.[20]

Pursuant to H.Res. 1013, the report on the Select Committee's activities at the end of the 89th Congress (1965-1966) included recommendations for House action on ethics-related matters. Because the select committee only existed between October and December 1966, the committee concluded that they could not "prudently recommend changes in existing provisions of law or recommend new ones at this time."[21] Instead, they recommended that (1) the committee be continued as a select committee in the 90th Congress; (2) legislation introduced in the 90th Congress on standards and conduct should be referred to the select committee; and (3) Members of the House should be asked for suggested changes in existing statutes. In addition, the report included draft language for the continuation of the select committee.[22]

(...continued)

S.Res. 2, 89th Cong., 2nd sess., S.Rept. 89-1414 (Washington: GPO, 1966), p. 48.

[17] "Public Bills and Resolutions," *Congressional Record*, vol. 112, part 16 (September 2, 1966), p. 21738.

[18] U.S. Congress, House, Committee on Rules, *Creating a Select Committee on Standards and Conduct*, report to accompany H.Res. 1013, 89th Cong., 2nd sess., September 7, 1966, H.Rept. 89-2012 (Washington: GPO, 1966); and Rep. Claude Pepper, "Creating a Select Committee on Standards and Conduct," remarks in the House, *Congressional Record*, vol. 112, part 16 (September 7, 1966), p. 21949.

[19] "Creating a Select Committee on Standards and Conduct," House debate, *Congressional Record*, vol. 112, part 20 (October 19, 1966), pp. 27713-27730.

[20] U.S. Congress, House, Select Committee on Standards and Conduct, *Report of the Select Committee on Standards and Conduct of the House of Representatives*, under the authority of H.Res. 1013, 89th Cong., 2nd sess., December 27, 1966, H.Rept. 89-2338 (Washington: GPO, 1966), p. vii.

[21] U.S. Congress, House, Select Committee on Standards and Conduct, *Report Under the Authority of H.Res. 1013*, 89th Cong., 2nd sess., H.Rept. 89-2338 (Washington: GPO, 1966), p. 1.

[22] Ibid.

Committee on Standards of Official Conduct (Now Committee on Ethics)

In the first session of the 90th Congress (1967-1966), more than 100 resolutions were introduced to create a Committee on Standards of Official Conduct. One of these proposals, H.Res. 18, was introduced on January 10, 1967, by Representative Charles Bennett, chair of the Select Committee on Standards and Conduct in the 89th Congress.[23] H.Res. 18 was referred to the Committee on Rules, which held a series of hearings on this, and other similar resolutions, in February and March 1967.[24]

During the hearings, the Committee on Rules heard from numerous Members of the House and considered proposals to create both a select and a standing committee on standards and conduct. Representative Bennett, the sponsor of H.Res. 18, argued that a standards committee would be essential to aid the House in dealing with issues of perceived and actual impropriety by Members. He testified:

> The public image of Congress demands that the House establish a full, working, thoughtful committee working solely in the field of standards and conduct. Sixty percent of those answering a recent Gallup poll said they believe the misuse of Government funds by Congressmen is fairly common. Of course, we know that such abuses are, in fact, not common, but we have seen a number of such damaging polls showing the people's lack of faith in the integrity of Congress.
>
> There is a need for a vehicle in the House to achieve and maintain the highest possible standards by statute and enforcement thereof. This can only be done after through study by a committee whose primary interests are in the field of ethics.[25]

On April 6, 1967, following its hearings on H.Res. 18 and other similar resolutions, the House Rules Committee reported H.Res. 418,[26] "to establish a standing committee to be known as the Committee on Standards of Official Conduct."[27]

---

[23] "Public Bills and Resolutions," *Congressional Record*, vol. 113, part 1 (January 10, 1967), p. 130.

[24] U.S. Congress, House, Committee on Rules, *Creating a Select Committee on Standards and Conduct*, hearing on H.Res. 18 and Similar Measures, 90th Cong., 1st sess., February 21 and 22, 1967 (Washington: GPO, 1967); U.S. Congress, House Committee on Rules, *Creating a Select Committee on Standards and Conduct: Part 2*, hearing on H.Res. 18 and similar measures, 90th Cong., 1st sess., February 28, 1967 (Washington: GPO, 1967); and U.S. Congress, House Committee on Rules, *Creating a Select Committee on Standards and Conduct: Part 3*, hearings on H.Res. 18 and similar measures, 90th Cong., 1st sess., March 7, 8, 14, and 15, 1967 (Washington: GPO, 1967).

[25] U.S. Congress, House, Committee on Rules, *Creating a Select Committee on Standards and Conduct*, hearing on H.Res. 18 and Similar Measures, 90th Cong., 1st sess., February 21 and 22, 1967 (Washington: GPO, 1967), p 8.

[26] U.S. Congress, House, Committee on Rules, *Establishing a Standing Committee to be Known as the Committee on Standards of Official Conduct, and for Other Purposes*, report to accompany H.Res. 418, 90th Cong., 1st sess., April 6, 1967, H.Rept. 90-178 (Washington: GPO, 1967). For more information on the Committee on Rules ability to issue privileged reports in the 90th Congress, see Rule XI, clause 22 (90th Congress) in U.S. Congress, House, *Constitution, Jefferson's Manual, and Rules of the House of Representatives of the United States Ninetieth Congress*, prepared by Lewis Deschler, Parliamentarian, 89th Cong., 2nd sess. (Washington: GPO, 1967), pp. 360-361.

[27] Rep. William Colmer, "To Establish a Standing Committee to be Known as the Committee on Standards of Official Conduct, and for Other Purposes," *Congressional Record*, vol. 113, part 7 (April 6, 1967), p. 8622; and Rep. William Colmer, "Establishing a Standing Committee on Standards and Conduct," *Journal of the House of Representatives of the United States*, 90th cong., 1st sess., (April 6, 1967), p. 463.

On April 13, the House debated and passed H.Res. 418 by a vote of 400 to zero.[28] The resolution created a bipartisan 12-member standing committee with the initial mission to make "recommendations for its jurisdiction"[29] and to "recommend as soon as practicable to the House of Representatives such changes in laws, rules, and regulations as the committee deems necessary to establish and enforce standards of official conduct for Members, officers and employees of the House."[30] The first members of the committee were appointed on May 1 when H.Res. 457 (majority members)[31] and H.Res. 458 (minority members)[32] were agreed to by the House.

The Committee on Standards of Official Conduct (Committee on Standards) held its first hearings in the summer and fall of 1967.[33] The hearings were designed to help the committee meet the requirements of H.Res. 418 "to write, and recommend to the House, a set of standards for the official conduct of the Chambers' Members and employees."[34]

In March 1968, the Committee issued a report summarizing their activities and recommending

- continuation of the committee as a select committee;

- changes in the committee's jurisdiction and powers;

- creation of a Code of Official Conduct and financial disclosure rules for Members, officers, and employees of the House;

- establishment of standardized controls by the Committee on House Administration over committees using counterpart funds (foreign currencies held by U.S. embassies that can only be spent in the country of origin);

- a prompt review of the Federal Corrupt Practices Act (reporting of campaign expenditures) by the House;[35] and

- compliance by House candidates with applicable provisions of the proposed Code of Official Conduct.[36]

---

[28] "Committee on Standards of Official Conduct," House debate, *Congressional Record*, vol. 113, part 7 (April 13, 1967), pp. 9426-9448.

[29] Ibid., p. 9426.

[30] "Committee on Standards of Official Conduct," *Journal of the House of Representatives of the United States*, 90th cong., 1st sess., (April 13, 1967), p. 488.

[31] Rep. Wilber Mills, "Election to Committee—Majority," *Journal of the House of Representatives of the United States*, 90th cong., 1st sess. (May 1, 1967), p. 539. The majority committee members were Representatives Melvin Price (chair), Olin Teague, Joe Evins, Watkins Abbitt, Wayne Aspinall, and Edna Kelly.

[32] Rep. Gerald Ford, "Election to Committee—Minority," *Journal of the House of Representatives of the United States*, 90th cong., 1st sess. (May 1, 1967), p. 539. The minority committee members were Representatives Charles Halleck, Leslie Arends, Jackson Betts, Robert Stafford, James Quillen, and Lawrence Williams.

[33] U.S. Congress, House, Committee on Standards of Official Conduct, *Standards of Official Conduct*, hearings, 90th Cong., 1st sess., August 16-17, 23-24, and September 14, 21, and 27, 1967 (Washington: GPO, 1967).

[34] Ibid., p. 1.

[35] The Corrupt Practices Act (P.L. 61-274, 36 Stat. 822, June 25, 1910) was repealed by the Federal Election Campaign Act in 1971 (P.L. 92-225, 86 Stat. 3, February 7, 1972; 2 U.S.C. §431 et seq., as amended). For more information on the Federal Election Campaign Act, see CRS Report R41542, *The State of Campaign Finance Policy: Recent Developments and Issues for Congress*, by R. Sam Garrett.

[36] U.S. Congress, House, Committee on Standards of Official Conduct, *Code of Conduct for Members and Employees of the House*, report under the authority of H.Res. 418, 90th Cong., 2nd sess., H.Rept. 90-1176 (Washington: GPO, 1968), pp. 7-11.

On March 14, 1968, Representative Melvin Price, chair of the Committee on Standards, introduced H.Res. 1099 "to continue the Committee on Standards of Official Conduct as a permanent standing committee of the House of Representatives."[37] The resolution was referred to the Committee on Rules, and was reported with amendments on April 1.[38] On April 3, the Committee on Rules reported a special rule (H.Res. 1119) for the consideration of H.Res. 1099. Following adoption of H.Res. 1119, debate on H.Res. 1099 proceeded. In his opening statement, Representative Price discussed the reasons for amending H.Res. 418 and making the committee a permanent, standing committee of the House.

> The reason for amending that original resolution, as opposed to offering a completely new resolution, is that the committee felt it would be advantageous—from the standpoints of continuity and orderliness—to extend the life of the existing committee rather than constitute a new committee.[39]

Following the adoption of several amendments, H.Res. 1099 was agreed to by a vote of 406 to 1.[40] The resolution provided for (1) continuation of the Committee on Standards as a permanent standing House committee; (2) enumeration of the committee's jurisdiction and powers; (3) creation of the first House Code of Official Conduct (Rule XLIII);[41] and (4) adoption of the first financial disclosure requirements for Members, officers, and designated employees (Rule XLIV).[42]

In the 112th Congress, the House renamed the Committee on Standards of Official Conduct to the Committee on Ethics.[43] The committee will be referred to as the Committee on Ethics for the remainder of this report.

---

[37] "Public Bills and Resolutions," *Congressional Record*, vol. 114, part 5 (March 14, 1968), p. 6503.

[38] U.S. Congress, House, Committee on Rules, *Amending H.Res. 418, 90th Congress, to Continue the Committee on Standards of Official Conduct as a Permanent Standing Committee of the House of Representatives, and for Other Purposes*, report to accompany H.Res. 1099, 90th Cong., 2nd sess., H.Rept. 90-1248 (Washington: GPO, 1968). See also "Reports of Committees on Public Bills and Resolutions," *Congressional Record*, vol. 114, part 7 (April 1, 1968), p. 8406.

[39] Rep. Melvin Price, "Standards of Official Conduct," House debate, *Congressional Record*, vol. 114, part 7 (April 3, 1968), p. 8778.

[40] Ibid., p. 8812.

[41] Rule XLIII is currently codified as Rule XXIII. For the original text of the Code of Official Conduct, see U.S. Congress, House, *Constitution, Jefferson's Manual, and Rules of the House of Representatives of the United States Ninety-First Congress*, Lewis Deschler, Parliamentarian, 90th Cong., 2nd sess., H.Doc. 90-402 (Washington: GPO, 1969), pp. 499a-499b. For current Code of Official Conduct language, see U.S. Congress, House, *Constitution, Jefferson's Manual, and Rules of the House of Representatives One Hundred Eleventh Congress of the United States*, John V. Sullivan, Parliamentarian, 110th Cong., 2nd sess., H.Doc. 110-162 (Washington: GPO, 2003), pp. 918-928; and CRS Report RL30764, *Enforcement of Congressional Rules of Conduct: An Historical Overview*, by Jacob R. Straus.

[42] H.Res. 1099 (90th Congress), agreed to April 3, 1968. Rule XLIV is currently codified as Rule XXVI. For the original text of Financial Disclosure requirements, see U.S. Congress, House, *Constitution, Jefferson's Manual, and Rules of the House of Representatives of the United States Ninety-First Congress*, Lewis Deschler, Parliamentarian, 90th Cong., 2nd sess., H.Doc. 90-402 (Washington: GPO, 1969), pp. 499c-499f. For current Code of Official Conduct language, see U.S. Congress, House, *Constitution, Jefferson's Manual, and Rules of the House of Representatives One Hundred Eleventh Congress of the United States*, John V. Sullivan, Parliamentarian, 110th Cong., 2nd sess., H.Doc. 110-162 (Washington: GPO, 2003), pp. 962-986.

[43] H.Res. 5 (112th Congress), agreed to January 5, 2011; "Rules of the House" *Congressional Record*, daily edition, vol. 157 (January 5, 2011), p. H7.

Jurisdiction

In addition to establishing the Committee on Ethics as a permanent standing committee, H.Res. 1099 formalized the committee's jurisdiction. The *History of the United States House of Representatives, 1789-1994*, published by the Committee on House Administration in the 103rd Congress (1993-1994), summarized four major jurisdictional areas for the Committee on Ethics.

> Since 1968, the House has authorized and directed the Ethics Committee to: (1) recommend to the House legislative or administrative actions deemed necessary for establishing or enforcing standards of conduct; (2) investigate allegations of violations of the Code of Official Conduct or any law, rule, regulation, or other standard of conduct applicable to Members, officers, and employees in the performance of official duties; and after notice and a hearing, recommend to the House whatever action or sanctions it deems appropriate; (3) subject to House approval, report to appropriate state and federal authorities about evidence of violations of law by Members, officers, and employees in the performance of official duties;[44] and (4) issue and publish advisory opinions for the guidance of Members, officers, and employees.[45]

The committee was also provided with jurisdiction over the Code of Official Conduct and financial disclosure.[46]

In addition to establishing the committee's jurisdiction, H.Res. 1099, and subsequent amendments, imposed several constraints on the Committee on Ethics. These limits, except where noted, are still in effect in House Rule XI, clause 3(a). They stipulate that

- there must be an affirmative vote of seven out of 12 committee members for the issuance of any report, resolution, recommendation, or advisory opinion relating to the official conduct of a Member, officer, or employee or the investigation of such conduct;[47]

- investigations, other than those initiated by the committee, can be undertaken only upon receipt of a complaint, in writing and under oath, from a Member of the House, or an individual not a Member if the committee finds that such complaint has been submitted by the individual to no fewer than three Members who have refused in writing to transmit the complaint to the committee;[48]

---

[44] With the adoption of H.Res. 168 (105th Congress) on September 18, 1997, the House voted to permit an affirmative vote of two-thirds of the full Standards Committee or the approval of the House for the referral of evidence of violations of law to the appropriate law enforcement authorities.

[45] U.S. Congress, Committee on House Administration, *History of the United States House of Representatives, 1789-1994*, 103rd Cong., 2nd sess., H.Doc. 103-324 (Washington: GPO, 1994), p. 298.

[46] Ibid.

[47] The seven Member requirement was replaced in 1974 with "an affirmative vote by a majority of the members of the committee" to accommodate any subsequent changes in the committee's size (H.Res. 998, agreed to October 8, 1974). In 1991, pursuant to the Ethics Reform Act of 1989, the membership was increased to 14. However, in 1997, with the adoption of the recommendation of the Ethics Reform Task Force (H.Res. 168), the membership was reduced to 10. Also in the 105th Congress (1997-1999), the House permitted the chair and ranking minority member to gather additional information or establish an investigative subcommittee for a properly filed complaint (H.Res. 168, Section 11, agreed to September 18, 1997).

[48] H.Res. 168 (105th Congress), agreed to September 18, 1997, changed the requirements for the filing of complaints by non-Members to require that such complaints be transmitted by a Member who "certifies in writing to the committee (continued...)

- investigations of alleged violations of any law or rule that was not in effect at the time of the alleged violation are prohibited;[49] and

- members of the committee are not eligible to participate in any committee proceeding relating to their official conduct.[50]

H.Res. 1099 also empowered the committee to hold hearings, receive testimony, and issue subpoenas in the course of conducting an investigation.[51]

When discussing the jurisdiction of House committees, it is important to note that the House Parliamentarian is the sole definitive authority on questions relating to the jurisdiction of the chamber's committees and should be consulted for a formal opinion on any specific procedural question.[52]

Changes in Jurisdiction

Since the establishment of the Committee on Ethics as a permanent standing committee, the committee's jurisdiction has been amended a number of times. Each of these changes "necessitated following experience under prior rules"[53] and reflected the changing nature of ethics enforcement in the House.

Lobbying and Campaign Finance

On May 19, 1970, Representative William Colmer introduced H.Res. 1031 to amend then clause 19 of Rule XI of the House "with respect of lobbying practices and political campaign contributions affecting the House of Representatives."[54] The Committee on Rules reported the

---

(...continued)

that he or she believes the information is submitted in good faith and warrants the review and consideration of the Committee."

[49] This rule was expanded by the Ethics Reform Act of 1989 to include a statute of limitations of three previous Congresses for investigations of alleged violations (P.L. 101-194, Section 803(g), 103 Stat. 1775, November 30, 1989).

[50] Committee rule 9, clauses (d) and (e) require that a committee Member under investigation or who has a conflict of interest with an investigation be excluded from those proceedings. The rule states: "(d) A member of the Committee shall be ineligible to participate in any Committee or subcommittee proceeding in which such Member is the respondent;" and "(e) A member of the Committee may seek disqualification from participating in any investigation of the conduct of a Member, officer, or employee of the House of Representatives upon the submission in writing and under oath of an affidavit of disqualification stating that the member cannot render an impartial and unbiased decision. If the Committee approves and accepts such affidavit of disqualification, the Chair shall so notify the Speaker and ask the Speaker to designate a Member of the House of Representatives from the same political party as the disqualified member of the Committee to act as a member of the Committee in any Committee proceeding relating to such investigation" (U.S. Congress, House, Committee on Standards of Official Conduct, *Rules*, 111th Cong., 1st sess., June 9, 2009 (http://ethics.house.gov/Media/PDF/111th_Rules_Amended_June_2009.pdf), pp. 16-17.

[51] U.S. Congress, Committee on House Administration, *History of the United States House of Representatives, 1789-1994*, 103rd Cong., 2nd sess., H.Doc. 103-324 (Washington: GPO, 1994), p. 298.

[52] For more information on the Parliamentarian of the House and the referral process, see CRS Report RS20544, *The Office of the Parliamentarian in the House and Senate*, by Valerie Heitshusen and CRS Report 98-175, *House Committee Jurisdiction and Referral: Rules and Practice*, by Judy Schneider.

[53] U.S. Congress, House, Committee on Standards of Official Conduct, *House Ethics Manual: 2008 Edition*, 110th Cong., 2nd sess. (Washington: GPO, 2008), p. 8.

[54] "Public Bills and Resolutions," *Congressional Record*, vol. 116, part. 12 (May 19, 1970), p. 16193.

---

resolution on June 11,[55] and it was brought up for debate on July 8. Following debate, the resolution was adopted to give the Committee on Ethics formal jurisdiction over lobbying activities as well as those involving the raising, reporting, and use of campaign funds.[56]

Authority over campaign contributions, lobbying, and financial disclosure have subsequently been removed from the committee's jurisdiction. In the 94th Congress (1975-1976), the House transferred jurisdiction over campaign contributions to the Committee on House Administration as part of the rules package.[57] In the 95th Congress (1977-1978), the House transferred jurisdiction over lobbying to the Committee on the Judiciary[58] and jurisdiction over measures relating to financial disclosure was reassigned to the Committee on Rules.[59]

Rules of Conduct

On March 2, 1977, the House adopted H.Res. 287, which contained several amendments and additions to the House rules of conduct.[60] Included were the first requirement that financial disclosure be made public; limits on outside earned income and unofficial office accounts; and further restrictions on the acceptance of gifts, the use of the franking privilege, and limits on foreign travel. Pursuant to H.Res. 287, the Committee on Ethics assumed jurisdiction over these additional areas and was authorized to maintain the public financial disclosure reports filed by Members, officers, and designated employees.[61] In addition, the House established a Select Committee on Ethics, chaired by Representative L. Richardson Preyer, to assist the Committee on Ethics with the implementation of the new rules.[62]

Additional Authorities

On July 14, 1977, the House agreed to H.Res. 658 and established the Permanent Select Committee on Intelligence.[63] The resolution also authorized the Committee on Ethics to

---

[55] U.S. Congress, House, Committee on Rules, *Amending Clause 19 of Rule XI of the Rules of the House of Representatives with Respect of Lobbying Practices and Political Campaign Contributions Affecting the House of Representatives and for Other Purposes*, report to accompany H.Res. 1031, 91st Cong., 2nd sess., June 11, 1970, H.Rept. 91-1186 (Washington: GPO, 1970).

[56] "Lobbying Practices and Political Campaign Contributions Affecting the House of Representatives," *Congressional Record*, vol. 116, part 17 (July 8, 1970), pp. 23136-23141.

[57] "Rules of the House," *Congressional Record*, vol. 121, part 1 (January 14, 1975), p. 20.

[58] "Establishing a Select Committee on Ethics," *Congressional Record*, vol. 123, part 6, (March 9, 1977), pp. 6811-6817.

[59] "Rules of the House," *Congressional Record*, vol. 123, January 4, 1977, p. 53. The committee continued to retain substantive jurisdiction over financial disclosure pursuant to the Ethics in Government Act of 1978 (P.L. 95-521, 92 Stat. 1824, October 26, 1978).

[60] "Providing for Consideration of House Resolution 287, to Amend the Rules of the House of Representatives," *Congressional Record*, vol. 123, part 5 (March 2, 1977), pp. 5885-5953.

[61] The Clerk of the House maintains the public repository for House financial disclosure reports pursuant to 5 U.S.C. app. §101 *et seq.* For more information on financial disclosure statements, see U.S. Congress, Clerk of the House of Representatives, "Financial Disclosure Reports," http://clerk.house.gov/public_disc/financial.html.

[62] H.Res. 383 (95th Congress). U.S. Congress, House Committee on Rules, *Establishing a Select Committee on Ethics*, report to accompany H.Res. 383, 95th Cong., 1st sess., March 8, 1977, H.Rept. 95-61 (Washington: GPO, 1977); and "Establishing a Select Committee on Ethics," *Congressional Record*, vol. 123, part 6 (March 9, 1977), pp. 6811-6817.

[63] "Amending the Rules of the House of Representatives and Establish a Permanent a Permanent Select Committee on Intelligence, *Congressional Record*, vol. 123, part 18 (July 14, 1977), pp. 22932-22949.

"investigate an unauthorized disclosure of intelligence or intelligence-related information by a Member, officer, or employee of the House in violation of paragraph (c) and report to the House concerning any allegation which it finds to be substantiated."[64]

In August 1977, the Committee on Ethics was designated at the "employing agency" for the House.[65] Pursuant to P.L. 95-105, the Foreign Relations Authorization Act for FY 1978, the Committee was authorized to issue regulations governing the acceptance by House Members, personnel, and employees of gifts, trips, and decorations from foreign governments.[66]

Financial Disclosure

In 1978, the Ethics in Government Act began requiring government-wide public financial disclosure requirements.[67] Subsequently, with the adoption of the House rules for the 96th Congress (1979-1980), the provisions of the House financial disclosure rule were replaced by those of the Ethics Act and incorporated into House rules.[68] This act delegated to the Committee on Ethics review, interpretation, and compliance responsibilities for the public financial disclosure reports that henceforth were to be filed with the Clerk of the House.

On April 4, 2012, the STOCK Act (Stop Trading on Congressional Knowledge Act) was passed to affirm that no exemption exists from "insider trading" laws and regulations for Members of Congress and congressional employees.[69] Pursuant to the act, the House Committee on Ethics (and the Senate Select Committee on Ethics) is required to

> issue interpretive guidance of the relevant rules of each chamber, including rules on conflicts of interest and gifts, clarifying that a Member of Congress and an employee of Congress may not use nonpublic information derived from such person's position as a Member of Congress or employee of Congress or gained from the performance of such person's official responsibilities as a means for making a private profit.[70]

On August 17, 2012, the committee issued a "pink sheet" on the implementation of the STOCK Act that clarified who is required to file, what transactions must be reported, the requirements for participating in a stock's initial public offering (IPO), waivers and exclusions to the act, when transactions must be reported, how and where transactions should be reported, late filing fees, penalties for failing to file and filing false information, and how to get assistance from the committee.[71]

---

[64] Ibid., p. 22934.

[65] P.L. 95-105, 91 Stat. 863, August 17, 1977.

[66] P.L. 95-105, 91 Stat. 864, August 17, 1977.

[67] P.L. 95-521, 92 Stat. 1824, October 26, 1978; 5 U.S.C. app. §101.

[68] "Rules of the House," *Congressional Record*, vol. 125, part 1 (January 15, 1979), p. 9.

[69] P.L. 112-105, 126 Stat. 291, April 4, 2012. The STOCK Act has been amended three times to change the effective date for financial disclosure forms required under the act. First, P.L. 112-173 (126 Stat. 1310, August 16, 2012) extended the filing date to September 30, 2012. Second, P.L. 112-178 (126 Stat. 1408, September 28, 2012) extended the required filing date to December 8, 2012. Finally, P.L. 112-207 (126 Stat. 1495, December 7, 2012) extended the required filing date to April 15, 2013. For a more detailed analysis of the STOCK Act, see CRS Report R42495, *The STOCK Act, Insider Trading, and Public Financial Reporting by Federal Officials*, by Jack Maskell.

[70] P.L. 112-105, Section 3; 5 U.S.C. app. 101 note prec.

[71] U.S. Congress, House Committee on Ethics, *Periodic Reporting of Personal Financial Transactions Pursuant to the STOCK Act, as amended*, 112th Cong., 2nd sess. (August 17, 2012), at http://ethics.house.gov/sites/ethics.house.gov/ (continued...)

Ethics Reform Act of 1989

The Ethics Reform Act of 1989 amended the Ethics in Government Act of 1978 and included a variety of ethics and pay reforms for the three branches of government. Enforcement of these changes further expanded the jurisdiction of the Committee on Ethics.[72] Changes made pursuant to the Ethics Reform Act of 1989 included enforcement of the act's ban on honoraria, limits on outside earned income, and restrictions on the acceptance of gifts. The committee was also given the responsibility for consideration of any requests for a written waiver of the limits imposed by the House gift ban rule.[73]

Procedures

Procedures for the Committee on Ethics are set through House Rule XI, clause 3 and are further specified in the committee's rules.[74]

Since its creation in 1967, several changes have been made to the Committee on Ethics' procedures. Change to the committee's procedures can be divided into six broad time periods or categories: changes in the 1970s, the Ethics Reform Act of 1989, the Ethics Reform Task Force of 1997, 109th Congress changes, 110th Congress changes, and the creation of the Office of Congressional Ethics in 2008.

Changes in the 1970s

During the first years of the Committee on Ethics many adjustments were made to the procedural operations of the committee. While some of the changes made during the 1970s have been repealed or replaced, three changes remain in effect.

1. In the 93rd Congress (1973-1974), the House agreed to H.Res. 988 and amended the jurisdiction and procedures of nearly all standing committees.[75] As part of those reforms, House Rules were amended to permit a majority vote to approve

---

(...continued)

files/PTR%20amended%20pink%20sheet.pdf

[72] P.L. 101-194, 103 Stat. 1716, November 30, 1989. The Ethics Reform Act, also mandated certain changes in the committee's procedures, *infra*. See U.S. Congress, House, *Report of the Bipartisan Task Force on Ethics* on *H.R. 3360*, committee print, 101st Cong., 1st sess. (Washington: GPO, 1989), pp. 9-11, 16-21; and "Government Ethics Reform Act of 1989," *Congressional Record*, vol. 135, part 21 (November 16, 1989), pp. 29469-29509.

[73] U.S. Congress, House Bipartisan Task Force on Ethics, *H.R. 3660, to Amend the Rules of the House of Representatives and the Ethics in Government Act of 1978 to Provide for Government-Wide Ethics Reform, and for Other Purposes*, committee print, 101st Cong., 1st sess., November 15, 1989 (Washington: GPO, 1989), pp. 4-5.

[74] U.S. Congress, House, *Constitution, Jefferson's Manual, and Rules of the House of Representatives One Hundred Eleventh Congress*, prepared by John V. Sullivan, Parliamentarian, 110th Cong., 2nd sess., H.Doc. 110-162 (Washington: GPO, 2009), §806, pp. 567-596; and U.S. Congress, House Committee on Standards of Official Conduct, *Rules*, 111th Cong., 1st sess., June 9, 2009 (http://ethics house.gov/Media/PDF/111th_Rules_Amended_June_2009.pdf).

[75] U.S. Congress, House, Select Committee on Committees, *Committee Reform Amendments of 1974*, report to accompany H.Res. 988, 93rd Cong., 2nd sess., March 19, 1974, H.Rept. 93-916, Part 1 (Washington: GPO, 1974); U.S. Congress, House Select Committee on Committees, *Committee Reform Amendments of 1974*, report to accompany H.Res. 988, 93rd Cong., 2nd sess., March 19, 1974, H.Rept. 93-916, Part 2 (Washington: GPO, 1974); and "Committee Reform Amendments of 1974," *Congressional Record*, vol. 120, part 26 (October 8, 1974), pp. 34447-34470.

Committee on Standard's reports, recommendations, advisory opinions, and investigations;[76]

2. In the 95th Congress (1977-1978), the House included in its opening day rules package a provision permitting a member of the committee to disqualify himself/herself from participating in an investigation upon submission of an affidavit of disqualification in writing and under oath;[77] and

3. In the 96th Congress (1979-1980), House rules were amended to prohibit "information or testimony received, or the contents of a complaint or the fact of its filing" from being "publicly disclosed by any committee or staff member unless specifically authorized in each instance by a vote of the full committee."[78]

Ethics Reform Act of 1989

The Ethics Reform Act of 1989 (P.L. 101-194) contained provisions affecting all three branches of government and mandated changes to the House Committee on Ethics.[79] Specifically, it established the Office of Advice and Education in the Committee on Ethics. The Office of Advice and Education's primarily responsibilities include

(A) Providing information and guidance to Members, officers and employees of the House regarding any laws, rules, regulations, and other standards of conduct applicable to such individuals in their official capacities, and any interpretations and advisory opinions of the committee.

(B) Submitting to the chairman and ranking minority member of the committee any written request from any such Member, officer or employee for an interpretation of applicable laws, rules, regulations, or other standards of conduct, together with any recommendations thereon.

(C) Recommending to the committee for its consideration formal advisory opinions of general applicability.

(D) Developing and carrying out, subject to the approval of the chairman, periodic educational briefings for Members, officers and employees of the House on those laws, rules, regulations, or other standards of conduct applicable to them.[80]

---

[76] U.S. Congress, House, Select Committee on Committees, *Committee Reform Amendments of 1974*, report to accompany H.Res. 988, 93rd Cong., 2nd sess., March 19, 1974, H.Rept. 93-916, Part 2 (Washington: GPO, 1974), p. 176. See also "Committee Reform Amendments of 1974," *Congressional Record*, vol. 120, part 26 (October 8, 1974), pp. 34406-34420; and "Committee Reform Amendments of 1974," *Congressional Record*, vol. 120, part 26 (October 8, 1974), pp. 34447-34470. Previously, an affirmative vote of 10 Members of the 12 Member panel were required for approving committee reports, issuing recommendations or advisory opinions, and initiating investigations. See footnote 47 for more information.

[77] "Rules of the House," *Congressional Record*, vol. 123, part 1 (January 4, 1977), p. 53.

[78] "Rules of the House," *Congressional Record*, vol. 125, part 1 (January 15, 1979), p. 8.

[79] P.L. 101-194, 103 Stat. 1716, November 30, 1989. For the debate on the Ethics Reform Act of 1989, see "Government Ethics Reform Act of 1989," House debate, *Congressional Record*, vol. 135, part 21, (November 16, 1989), pp. 29468-29513; "Government Ethics Reform Act of 1989," Senate debate, *Congressional Record*, vol. 135, part 21, (November 17, 1989), pp. 29660-29678; and 29681-29707; and "Government Ethics Reform Act," Senate debate, *Congressional Record*, vol. 135, part 21 (November 17, 1979), pp. 29777-29796.

[80] P.L. 101-194, Section 803(i), 103 Stat. 1775, November 30, 1989; 2 U.S.C. §29d.

The Office of Advice and Education offers training, guidance, and provides recommendations to Members, officers, and employees of the House on standards of conduct applicable to their official duties.[81]

Many other changes implemented by the 1989 act are still applicable. These include

- "bifurcation" (separation) within the committee of its investigative and adjudicative functions;[82]

- a requirement that the committee report to the House on any case it has voted to investigate and that any "letter of reproval" or other committee administrative action may be issued only as part of a final report to the House;[83]

- a statute of limitation prohibiting the committee from initiating or undertaking an investigation of alleged violations occurring prior to the third previous Congress unless they are related to a continuous course of conduct in recent years;[84]

- a guarantee that any Member who is the respondent in any Ethics Committee investigation may be accompanied by one counsel on the House floor during consideration of his/her case;[85] and

- a time limit of committee service of no more than three out of any five consecutive Congresses.[86]

The act also increased the size of the committee's membership from 12 to 14.[87] That change, however, was superseded by the 1997 amendments that reduced the size of the committee from 14 to 10 members.[88]

---

[81] For more information on the Office of Advice and Education, see U.S. Congress, House, Committee on Ethics, "About: Committee Advice," 111th Cong., 2nd sess. (http://ethics house.gov/About/Default.aspx?Section=8); and U.S. Congress, House, Committee on Standards of Official Conduct, *Summary of Activities, One Hundred Tenth Congress*, 110th Cong., 2nd sess., January 3, 2009, H.Rept. 110-938 (Washington: GPO, 2009).

[82] Bifurcation is the separation of administrative and investigative functions of the Committee on Ethics. The Ethics Task Force defined bifurcation as: "... a 'firewall' between the Committee functions of investigation and adjudication, ensuring that Committee members who charge a respondent with a violation do not also participate in a judgment of whether liability has been established. It also allocates responsibility within the Committee so that the review of information offered as a complaint is less time-consuming for members of the Committee and is consistent with the confidentiality imposed on the complaint process. For these reasons, the Task Force encourages Committee members to protect the integrity of the 'firewall' to the greatest degree possible." See U.S. Congress, House, Committee on Rules, *Report of the Ethics Reform Task Force on H.Res. 168*, committee print, 105th Cong., 1st sess., June 17, 1997 (Washington: GPO, 1997), p. 7.

[83] P.L. 101-194, Section 803(e), 103 Stat. 1774, November 30, 1989.

[84] P.L. 101-194, Section 803(g), 103 Stat. 1775, November 30, 1989.

[85] Ibid. For information on "Letters of Reproval," see CRS Report RL30764, *Enforcement of Congressional Rules of Conduct: An Historical Overview*, by Jacob R. Straus.

[86] P.L. 101-194, Section 803(a), 103 Stat. 1773, November 30, 1989. House Rule X, clause 5. Democratic Caucus Rules include additional limits on committee service.

[87] P.L. 101-194, 103 Stat. 1774, November 30, 1989; 2 U.S.C. §29d.

[88] "Implementing the Recommendations of Bipartisan House Ethics Task Force," *Congressional Record*, vol. 143, September 18, 1997, pp. 19302-19340.

Ethics Reform Task Force

On February 12, 1997, the House created an Ethics Reform Task Force to "look into any and all aspects of the ethics process," including:

> Who can file a complaint and upon what basis of information, what should be the standards for initiating an investigation, what evidentiary standard should apply throughout the process, how has the bifurcation process worked, does it take too long to conduct a review, should non-House Members play a part in a reformed ethics process, should we enlarge the pool of Members who might participate in different phases of the process?[89]

Chaired by Representatives Bob Livingston and Ben Cardin, the 10-member task force was directed to review the existing House ethics process and to recommend reforms.[90] At the same time that the House approved the establishment of the task force, it also approved a 65-day moratorium on the filing of new ethics complaints to enable the Task Force to conduct its work "in a climate free from specific questions of ethical propriety."[91]

After seven months of study, the Task Force reported to the House in June 1997 with several recommendations. These included ensuring that the Committee on Standards operated in a non-partisan manner; that the committee's workings be kept confidential unless otherwise voted on by the committee; that an improved system be created for the filing of information offered as a complaint; that the committee should create an efficient administrative structure; that due process for Members, officers, and employees of the House be preserved; that Members play a greater role in the ethics process; and that matters before the committee be dealt with in a timely manner.[92]

On September 18, 1997, the House debated and agreed to H.Res. 230, a rule to provide for the consideration of H.Res. 168, the implementation of the Task Force's recommendations,[93] and proceeded to debate and amend H.Res. 168.[94] The major ethics process changes adopted pursuant to H.Res. 168 included the following:

- altering the way individuals who are not Members of the House file complaints with the Committee on Ethics by requiring them to have a Member of the House certify in writing that the information is submitted in good faith and warrants consideration;[95]

---

[89] Rep. Richard Armey, "Creation of Bipartisan Task Force to Review Ethics Process," *Congressional Record*, vol. 143, part 2 (February 12, 1997), p. 2059.

[90] "Creation of Bipartisan Task Force to Review Ethics Process," *Congressional Record*, vol. 143, part 2 (February 12, 1997), pp. 2058-2059.

[91] Rep. Richard Armey, "Creation of Bipartisan Task Force to Review Ethics Process," *Congressional Record*, vol. 143, part 2 (February 12, 1997), p. 2059.

[92] U.S. Congress, House Ethics Reform Task Force on H.Res. 168, *Recommending Revisions to the Rules of the House and the Rules of the Committee on Standards of Official Conduct with Additional Views*, committee print, 105th Cong., 1st sess., June 17, 1997 (Washington: GPO, 1997), pp. 4-5.

[93] "Providing for Consideration of H.Res. 168, Implementing the Recommendations of Bipartisan House Ethics Reform Task Force," *Congressional Record*, vol. 143, part 13 (September 18, 1997), pp. 19302-19310.

[94] "Implementing the Recommendations of Bipartisan House Ethics Task Force," *Congressional Record*, vol. 143, part 13 (September 18, 1997), pp. 19310-19340.

[95] H.Res. 168, Section 9 (105th Congress), agreed to September 17, 1997. This procedure superseded a process whereby non-House Members could file complaints with the Committee on Standards only after submitting allegations to at (continued...)

- decreasing the size of the committee from 14 members to 10;[96]

- establishing a 20-person pool of Members (10 from each party) to supplement the work of the Ethics Committee as potential appointees to investigative subcommittees that the committee might establish; [97]

- requiring the chair and ranking minority member of the committee to determine within 14 calendar days or 5 legislative days, whichever comes first, if the information offered as a complaint meets the committee's requirements;[98]

- allowing an affirmative vote of two-thirds of the members of the committee or approval of the full House to refer evidence of violations of law disclosed in a committee investigation to the appropriate state or federal law enforcement authorities;[99]

- providing for a nonpartisan, professional committee staff;[100]

- allowing the ranking minority member on the committee to place matters on the committee's agenda;[101] and

- decreasing the maximum service on the committee from six years to four years during any three successive Congresses and required at least four members to be rotated off the committee at the end of each Congress.[102]

109th Congress Changes

On January 4, 2005, the House included several provisions in its rules for the 109th Congress (2005-2006) that affected the Committee on Ethics. These included the process for handling

---

(...continued)

least three House Members, who had refused in writing to transmit the complaint to the committee.

[96] "Rules of the House," *Congressional Record*, vol. 145, part 1 (January 6, 1999), p. 54. The formal change in membership from 12 to 10 codified the defacto size of the committee in the 105th Congress even though the Ethics Reform Act of 1989 required each party to nominate seven Members for the committee (P.L. 101-194, Section 803(b), 103 Stat. 1774, November 30, 1989; 2 U.S.C. §29d).

[97] H.Res. 168, Section 1(a) (105th Congress), agreed to September 17, 1997. The first pool of 20 Members selected to serve on investigative committees of the Standards Committee was appointed on November 13, 1997. For a list of initial appointments, see Speaker Pro Tempore [Rep. Ray La Hood], "List of Republican and Democratic Members Selected to Serve As 'Pool' For Purposes Relating To The Committee on Standards of Official Conduct," *Congressional Record*, vol. 143, November 13, 1997, p. 26569. The House leadership has subsequently appointed a 20-person pool of Members in each Congress.

[98] H.Res. 168, Section 10 (105th Congress), agreed to September 17, 1997. Previously, there was no specific time limit for this determination.

[99] H.Res. 168, Section 18 (105th Congress), agreed to September 17, 1997. With the exception of a brief period in 1966, only a vote by the full House previously permitted referrals of possible violations of law to the appropriate authorities.

[100] H.Res. 168, Section 4 (105th Congress), agreed to September 17, 1997.

[101] H.Res. 168, Section 3 and Section 11 (105th Congress), agreed to September 17, 1997.

[102] H.Res. 168, Section 2 (105th Congress), agreed to September 17, 1997. When the House adopted its rules for the 106th Congress (1999-2001), it changed the committee service rule and also voted to eliminate the rule requiring four members of the Standards Committee to rotate off the committee every Congress. This action returned the committee's service requirement to what it had been after the adoption of the Ethics Reform Act of 1989 (no more than three Congresses in any period of five successive Congresses). See "Rules of the House," *Congressional Record*, vol. 145, part 1 (January 6, 1999), p. 54. House Democratic Caucus Rules further limit service on the Committee on Standards.

---

allegations against a House Member, officer, or employee; procedures for instances when the conduct of one Member, officer, or employee might be referenced in the course of an investigation against another Member, officer, or employee; the due process for respondents and witnesses; and the dismissal of complaints.[103] Subsequently, on April 27, 2005, the House reversed earlier 109th Congress changes when it agreed to H.Res. 240 and reinstated "certain provisions of the rules relating to procedures of the Committee on Standards of Official Conduct to the form in which those provisions existed at the close of the 108th Congress."[104]

110th Congress Changes

On June 5, 2007, the House agreed to H.Res. 451, directing the Committee on Ethics to "respond to the indictment of, or the filing of charges of criminal conduct in a court of the United States or any State against, any Member of the House of Representatives by empanelling an investigative subcommittee to review the allegations not later than 30 days after the date the Member is indicted or the charges are filed."[105] The resolution was adopted following the grand jury indictment of a Member of the House in the United States District Court for the Eastern District of Virginia. The requirements of H.Res. 451 were continued in the rules packages for both the 111th and the 112th Congresses.[106]

113th Congress Changes

As part of the rules package (H.Res. 5) for the 113th Congress (2013-2014), the House amended the Code of Conduct (Rule XXIII, clause 8(c)) to remove references to "spouses" and replace those references with the term "relative." For the purpose of the Rule, relative is defined as

> an individual who is related to the Member, Delegate, or Resident Commissioner as father, mother, son, daughter, brother, sister, uncle, aunt, first cousin, nephew, niece, husband, wife, father-in-law, mother-in-law, son-in-law, daughter-in-law, brother-in-law, sister-in-law, stepfather, stepmother, stepson, stepdaughter, stepbrother, stepsister, half brother, half sister, grandson, or granddaughter.[107]

Additionally, H.Res. 5 required that copies of executed oaths (or affirmations) made by an officer or employee of the House be retained by the Sergeant at Arms, while oaths (or affirmations) made by Members, Delegates, or the Resident Commissioner continue to be retained by the Clerk of the House.[108]

---

[103] "Rules of the House," *Congressional Record*, daily edition, vol. 151(January 4, 2005), pp. H8-H10.

[104] H.Res. 240 (109th Congress), agreed to April 27, 2005 with the adoption of H.Res. 241. "Amending the Rules of the House of Representatives to Reinstate Certain Provision of the Rules Relating to Procedures of the Committee on Standards of Official Conduct to the Form in which those Provisions Existed at the Close of the 108th Congress," *Congressional Record*, daily edition, vol. 151 (April 27, 2005), pp. H2616-H2626.

[105] H.Res. 451 (110th Congress), agreed to June 5, 2007.

[106] H.Res. 5 (111th Congress), agreed to January 6, 2009; "Rules of the House," *Congressional Record*, vol. 155 (January 6, 2009), p. H6-H10. H.Res. 5 (112th Congress), agreed to January 5, 2011; "Rules of the House," *Congressional Record*, daily edition, vol. 157 (January 5, 2011), p. H7.

[107] H.Res. 5, Section 2(e)(2), (113th Congress), agreed to on January 3, 2013; "Rules of the House," *Congressional Record*, daily edition, vol. 159 (January 3, 2013), p. H6.

[108] H.Res. 5, Section 2(e)(3), (113th Congress), agreed to January 3, 2013.

Office of Congressional Ethics

In January 2007, Speaker of the House Nancy Pelosi and Minority Leader John Boehner jointly established a Special Task Force on Ethics Enforcement in the House of Representatives.[109] Chaired by Representative Michael Capuano, the task force was charged with considering "whether the House should create an outside enforcement entity, based on examples in state legislatures and private entities."[110]

In December 2007, Chairman Capuano released a report and introduced H.Res. 895 to create an office of congressional ethics, composed of six board members jointly appointed by House leaders.[111] On March 11, 2008, the House adopted H.Res. 895 and created the Office of Congressional Ethics (OCE).[112] The first OCE board members were appointed in July 2008.[113]

The OCE held its first public meeting on January 23, 2009, and began to implement the structural requirements of H.Res. 895. It also adopted rules of procedure, a code of conduct, and rules for the conduct of a review. The Office of Congressional Ethics (OCE) was reauthorized by the House as part of the rules package (H.Res. 5) adopted by the 113th Congress on January 3, 2013.[114]

---

[109] U.S. Congress, Speaker of the House of Representatives, "Pelosi Announces Special Task Force on Ethics Enforcement," press release, January 31, 2007, http://speaker.house.gov/newsroom/pressreleases?id=0057.

[110] The other Members of the task force were Representatives Bobby Scott, Marty Meehan, Betty McCollum, Lamar Smith (ranking member), Dave Camp, Dave Hobson, and Todd Tiahrt. Representative David Price was appointed to the task force in July 2007, when Representative Meehan resigned from Congress.

[111] U.S. Congress, House Special Task Force on Ethics Enforcement, *Report of the Democratic Members of the Special Task Force on Ethics Enforcement*, committee print, 110th Cong., 1st sess., H.Prt. 110-1 (Washington: GPO, 2007), pp. 4-5. Subsequently, on February 27, 2008, ranking member Rep. Lamar Smith and the other Republican Members of the task force introduced H.Res. 1003, to provide increased accountability and transparency in the Committee on Standards of Official Conduct. On March 3, 2008, Representative Capuano also released proposed amendments to H.Res. 895. For more information on the proposed amendments, see Rep. Michael E. Capuano, "Amendments to the Proposed Reforms to the Ethics Process," Dear Colleague letter, March 3, 2008, http://www house.gov/capuano/news/2008/pr121907-letter030308.pdf.

[112] "Establishing an Office of Congressional Ethics," *Congressional Record*, daily edition, vol. 154 (March 11, 2008), pp. H1515-H1536.

[113] U.S. Congress, Speaker of the House of Representatives, "Pelosi, Boehner Announce Appointments to New Office of Congressional Ethics," press release, July 24, 2008, http://speaker.house.gov/newsroom/pressreleases?id=0762. The members are former Representatives David Skaggs (chair), Porter Goss (vice chair), Karan English, and Yvonne Brathwaite Burke; former House Chief Administrative Officer Jay Eagen; and former professor and chief of staff of the Federal Election Commission Allison Hayward. The alternates are former Representative and federal judge Abner Mikva and former Representative Bill Frenzel. Board members are appointed at the beginning of each Congress.

[114] H.Res. 5, Section 4(d), (113th Congress), agreed to January 3, 2013; "Rules of the House" *Congressional Record*, daily edition, vol. 159 (January 3, 2013), p. H6. For more information on the Office of Congressional Ethics, see CRS Report R40760, *House Office of Congressional Ethics: History, Authority, and Procedures*, by Jacob R. Straus.

Appendix. Membership on the Committee on Ethics, 1967-2013

Since its inception in the 90th Congress (1967-1968), the Committee on Ethics has had a total of 284 members.[115] **Table A-1** provides a list of all Members to have served on the Committee on Ethics, their party affiliation, and their state and district.

Table A-1. Congressional Committee Assignments: House Committee on Ethics

Member	Party	State	District
90th Congress (1967-1968)			
Price, C. Melvin	D	IL	24th
Teague, Olin E.	D	TX	6th
Evins, Joseph L.	D	TN	4th
Abbitt, Watkins M.	D	VA	4th
Aspinall, Wayne N.	D	CO	4th
Kelly, Edna F.	D	NY	12th
Halleck, Charles A.	R	IN	2nd
Arends, Leslie C.	R	IL	17th
Betts, Jackson E.	R	OH	8th
Stafford, Robert T.	R	VT	AL [a]
Quillen, James H.	R	TN	1st
Williams, Lawrence G.	R	PA	7th
91st Congress (1969-1970)			
Price, C. Melvin	D	IL	24th
Teague, Olin E.	D	TX	6th
Abbitt, Watkins M.	D	VA	4th
Aspinall, Wayne N.	D	CO	4th
Hébert, F. Edward	D	LA	1st
Holifield, Chet	D	CA	19th
Arends, Leslie C.	R	IL	17th
Betts, Jackson E.	R	OH	8th
Stafford, Robert T.	R	VT	AL [a]
Quillen, James H.	R	TN	1st

---

[115] Because all Members must be reappointed to the committee in subsequent Congress, this total counts Members who served in more than one Congress multiple times. The number of Members on the committee has fluctuated over time as the result of Members leaving the committee or being temporarily replaced due to conflict of interest for cases before the committee.

Member	Party	State	District
Williams, Lawrence G.	R	PA	7th
Hutchinson, Edward	R	MI	4th
Reid, Charlotte T.	R	IL	15th
92nd Congress (1971-1972)			
Price, C. Melvin	D	IL	24th
Teague, Olin E.	D	TX	6th
Abbitt, Watkins M.	D	VA	4th
Aspinall, Wayne N.	D	CO	4th
Hébert, F. Edward	D	LA	1st
Holifield, Chet	D	CA	19th
Betts, Jackson E.	R	OH	8th
Stafford, Robert T.	R	VT	AL [a]
Quillen, James H.	R	TN	1st
Williams, Lawrence G.	R	PA	7th
Hutchinson, Edward	R	MI	4th
Reid, Charlotte T.	R	IL	15th
King, Carleton J.	R	NY	30th
Spence, Floyd D.	R	SC	2nd
93rd Congress (1973-1974)			
Price, C. Melvin	D	IL	23rd
Teague, Olin E.	D	TX	6th
Hébert, F. Edward	D	LA	1st
Holifield, Chet	D	CA	19th
Flynt, John James Jr.	D	GA	6th
Foley, Thomas S.	D	WA	5th
Quillen, James H.	R	TN	1st
Williams, Lawrence G.	R	PA	7th
Hutchinson, Edward	R	MI	4th
King, Carleton J.	R	NY	29th
Spence, Floyd D.	R	SC	2nd
Hunt, John E.	R	NJ	1st
94th Congress (1975-1976)			
Price, C. Melvin	D	IL	23rd
Teague, Olin E.	D	TX	6th
Hébert, F. Edward	D	LA	1st
Flynt, John James Jr.	D	GA	6th

Member	Party	State	District
Foley, Thomas S.	D	WA	5th
Bennett, Charles E.	D	FL	3rd
Spence, Floyd D.	R	SC	2nd
Quillen, James H.	R	TN	1st
Hutchinson, Edward	R	MI	4th
Quie, Albert H.	R	MN	1st
Mitchell, Donald J.	R	NY	31st
Cochran, Thad	R	MS	4th

95th Congress (1977-1978)

Flynt, John James Jr.	D	GA	6th
Teague, Olin E.	D	TX	6th
Bennett, Charles E	D	FL	3rd
Hamilton, Lee H.	D	IN	9th
Preyer, L. Richardson	D	NC	6th
Flowers, Walter	D	AL	7th
Spence, Floyd D.	R	SC	2nd
Quillen, James H.	R	TN	1st
Quie, Albert H.	R	MN	1st
Cochran, Thad	R	MS	4th
Fenwick, Millicent H.	R	NJ	5th
Caputo, Bruce F.	R	NY	23rd

96th Congress (1979-1980)

Bennett, Charles E.	D	FL	3rd
Hamilton, Lee H.	D	IN	9th
Preyer, L. Richardson	D	NC	6th
Slack, John M. Jr.	D	WV	3rd
Murphy, Morgan F.	D	IL	2nd
Murtha, John P. Jr.	D	PA	12th
Spence, Floyd D.	R	SC	2nd
Hollenbeck, Harold C.	R	NJ	9th
Livingston, Robert L.	R	LA	1st
Thomas, William M.	R	CA	18th
Sensenbrenner, F. James Jr.	R	WI	9th
Cheney, Richard B.	R	WY	AL [a]
Stokes, Louis	D	OH	21st
Rahall, Nick J. II	D	WV	4th

Member	Party	State	District
97th Congress (1981-1982)			
Stokes, Louis	D	OH	21st
Rahall, Nick J. II	D	WV	4th
Alexander, William V. Jr.	D	AR	1st
Wilson, Charles	D	TX	2nd
Holland, Kenneth L.	D	SC	5th
Bailey, Donald A.	D	PA	21st
Spence, Floyd d.	R	SC	2nd
Conable, Barber B. Jr.	R	NY	35th
Myers, John T.	R	IN	7th
Forsythe, Edwin B.	R	NJ	6th
Brown, Hank	R	CO	4th
Hansen, James V.	R	UT	1st
98th Congress (1983-1984)			
Stokes, Louis	D	OH	21st
Rahall, Nick J. II	D	WV	4th
Jenkins, Edgar L.	D	GA	9th
Dixon, Julian C.	D	CA	28th
Fazio, Victor H.	D	CA	4th
Coyne, William J.	D	PA	14th
Spence, Floyd D.	R	SC	2nd
Conable, Barber B. Jr.	R	NY	30th
Myers, John T.	R	IN	7th
Forsythe, Edwin B.	R	NJ	13th
Brown, Hank	R	CO	4th
Hansen, James V.	R	UT	1st
Bliley, Thomas J. Jr.	R	VA	3rd
99th Congress (1985-1986)			
Dixon, Julian C.	D	CA	28th
Jenkins, Edgar L.	D	GA	9th
Fazio, Victor H.	D	CA	4th
Coyne, William J.	D	PA	14th
Dwyer, Bernard J.	D	NJ	6th
Mollohan, Alan B.	D	WV	1st
Spence, Floyd D.	R	SC	2nd
Myers, John T.	R	IN	7th

Member	Party	State	District
Hansen, James V.	R	UT	1st
Whitehurst, G. William	R	VA	2nd
Pursell, Carl D.	R	MI	2nd
Wortley, George	R	NY	27th

100th Congress (1987-1988)

Member	Party	State	District
Dixon, Julian C.	D	CA	28th
Fazio, Victor H.	D	CA	4th
Dwyer, Bernard J.	D	NJ	6th
Mollohan, Alan B.	D	WV	1st
Gaydos, Joseph M.	D	PA	20th
Atkins, Chester G.	D	MA	5th
Spence, Floyd	R	SC	2nd
Myers, John T.	R	IN	7th
Hansen, James V.	R	UT	1st
Pashayan, Charles S. Jr.	R	CA	17th
Petri, Thomas E.	R	WI	6th
Craig, Larry E.	R	ID	1st
Brown, Hank	R	CO	4th

101st Congress (1989-1990)

Member	Party	State	District
Dixon, Julian C.	D	CA	29th
Fazio, Victor H.	D	CA	4th
Dwyer, Bernard J.	D	NJ	6th
Mollohan, Alan B.	D	WV	1st
Gaydos, Joseph M.	D	PA	20th
Atkins, Chester G.	D	MA	5th
Stokes, Louis [b]	D	OH	21st
Myers, John T.	R	IN	7th
Hansen, James V.	R	UT	1st
Pashayan, Charles S. Jr.	R	CA	17th
Petri, Thomas E.	R	WI	6th
Craig, Larry E.	R	ID	1st
Grandy, Fred	R	IA	6th

102nd Congress (1991-1992)

Member	Party	State	District
Stokes, Louis	D	OH	21st
Ackerman, Gary L.	D	NY	7th
Darden, George (Buddy)	D	GA	7th

Member	Party	State	District
Cardin, Benjamin L.	D	MD	3rd
Pelosi, Nancy	D	CA	5th
McDermott, Jim	D	WA	7th
Mfume, Kweisi c	D	MD	7th
Hansen, James V.	R	UT	1st
Grandy, Fred	R	IA	6th
Johnson, Nancy L.	R	CT	6th
Bunning, Jim	R	KY	4th
Kyl, Jon L.	R	AZ	4th
Goss, Porter J.	R	FL	13th
Hobson, David L.	R	OH	7th
103rd Congress (1993-1994)			
McDermott, Jim	D	WA	7th
Darden, George (Buddy)	D	GA	7th
Cardin, Benjamim L.	D	MD	3rd
Pelosi, Nancy	D	CA	5th
Mfume, Kweisi	D	MD	7th
Borski, Robert A.	D	PA	3rd
Sawyer, Thomas C.	D	OH	14th
Grandy, Fred	R	IA	6th
Johnson, Nancy L.	R	CT	6th
Bunning, Jim	R	KY	4th
Kyl, Jon L.	R	AZ	4th
Goss, Porter J.	R	FL	13th
Hobson, David L.	R	OH	7th
Schiff, Steven	R	NY	1st
104th Congress (1995-1996) d			
Johnson, Nancy L.	R	CT	6th
Bunning, Jim	R	KY	4th
Goss, Porter J.	R	FL	13th
Hobson, David L.	R	OH	7th
Schiff, Steven	R	NM	1st
Smith, Lamar S. e	R	TX	21st
McDermott, Jim f	D	WA	7th
Cardin, Benjamin L.	D	MD	3rd
Pelosi, Nancy	D	CA	5th
Borski, Robert A.	D	PA	3rd

Member	Party	State	District
Sawyer, Thomas C.	D	OH	14th
105th Congress (1997-1998)			
Hansen, James V.	R	UT	1st
Smith, Lamar S.	R	TX	21st
Hefley, Joel	R	CO	5th
Goodlatte, Robert	R	VA	6th
Knollenberg, Joe	R	MI	11th
Berman, Howard L.	D	CA	26th
Sabo, Martin O.	D	MN	5th
Pastor, Ed	D	AZ	2nd
Fattah, Chaka	D	PA	2nd
Lofgren, Zoe	D	CA	16th
106th Congress (1999-2000)			
Smith, Lamar S.	R	TX	21st
Hefley, Joel	R	CO	5th
Knollenberg, Joe	R	MI	11th
Portman, Robert J.	R	OH	2nd
Camp, Dave	R	MI	4th
Berman, Howard L.	D	CA	26th
Sabo, Martin O.	D	MN	5th
Pastor, Ed	D	AZ	2nd
Fattah, Chaka	D	PA	2nd
Lofgren, Zoe	D	CA	16th
107th Congress (2001-2002)			
Hefley, Joel	R	CO	5th
Portman, Robert J.	R	OH	2nd
Hastings, Doc	R	WA	4th
Hutchison, Asa	R	AR	3rd
Biggert, Judy	R	IL	13th
Hulshof, Kenny	R	MO	9th
LaTourette, Steve	R	OH	19th
Berman, Howard	D	CA	26th
Sabo, Martin O.	D	MN	5th
Pastor, Ed	D	AZ	2nd
Lofgren, Zoe	D	CA	16th
Jones, Stephanie Tubbs	D	OH	11th

Member	Party	State	District
Green, Gene	D	TX	29th

108th Congress (2003-2004)

Member	Party	State	District
Hefley, Joel	R	CO	5th
Hastings, Doc	R	WA	4th
Biggert, Judy	R	IL	13th
Hulshof, Kenny	R	MO	9th
LaTourette, Steve	R	OH	19th
Berman, Howard	D	CA	26th
Mollohan, Alan B.	D	WV	1st
Jones, Stephanie Tubbs	D	OH	11th
Green, Gene	D	TX	29th
Roybal-Allard, Lucille	D	CA	34th
Doyle, Michael F.	D	PA	14th

109th Congress (2005-2006)

Member	Party	State	District
Hastings, Doc	R	WA	4th
Biggert, Judy	R	IL	13th
Smith, Lamar S.	R	TX	21st
Hart, Melissa	R	TX	4th
Cole, Tom	R	OK	4th
Mollohan, Alan B.	D	WV	1st
Berman, Howard, L. [g]	D	CA	28th
Jones, Stephanie Tubbs	D	OH	11th
Green, Gene	D	TX	29th
Roybal-Allard, Lucille	D	CA	34th
Doyle, Michael F.	D	PA	14th

110th Congress (2007-2008)

Member	Party	State	District
Jones, Stephanie Tubbs[h]	D	OH	11th
Green, Gene	D	TX	29th
Roybal-Allard, Lucille	D	CA	34th
Doyle, Michael F.	D	PA	14th
Delahunt, William D.	D	MA	10th
Scott, Robert C. "Bobby"	D	VA	3rd
Hastings, Doc	R	WA	4th
Bonner, Jo	R	AL	1st
Barrett, J. Gresham	R	SC	3rd
Kline, John	R	MN	2nd

Member	Party	State	District
McCaul, Michael T.	R	TX	10th

111th Congress (2009-2010)

Member	Party	State	District
Lofgren, Zoe	D	CA	16th
Chandler, Ben	D	KY	6th
Butterfield, G.K.	D	NC	1st
Castor, Kathy	D	FL	11th
Welch, Peter	D	VT	AL [a]
Bonner, Jo	R	AL	1st
Conaway, K. Michael	R	TX	11th
Dent, Charles W.	R	PA	15th
Harper, Gregg	R	MS	3rd
McCaul, Michael T.	R	TX	10th

112th Congress (2011-2012)

Member	Party	State	District
Bonner, Jo	R	AL	1st
McCaul, Michael T.	R	TX	10th
Conaway, K. Michael	R	TX	11th
Dent, Charles W.	R	PA	15th
Harper, Gregg	R	MS	3rd
Lofgren, Zoe [i]	D	CA	16th
Sánchez, Linda	D	CA	39th
Hirono, Mazie [j]	D	HI	2nd
Yarmuth, John	D	KY	3rd
Edwards, Donna	D	MD	4th
Pierluisi, Pedro	D	PR	AL [k]
Courtney, Joe [l]	D	CT	2nd

113th Congress (2013-2014)

Member	Party	State	District
Conaway, K. Michael	R	TX	11th
Dent, Charles W.	R	PA	15th
Meehan, Patrick	R	PA	7th
Gowdy, Trey	R	SC	4th
Brooks, Susan	R	IN	5th
Sánchez, Linda T.	D	CA	39th
Pierluisi, Pedro	D	PR	AL
Capuano, Michael E.	D	MA	7th
Clarke, Yvette D.	D	NY	9th
Deutch, Ted	D	FL	21st

Source: Garrison Nelson, Mary T. Mitchell, and Clark H. Bensen, *Committees in the U.S. Congress: 1947-1992* (Washington: CQ Press, 1994); U.S. Congress, Joint Committee on Printing, *1993-1994 Official Congressional Directory: 103rd Congress*, 103rd Cong., 1st sess., S.Pub. 103-8 (Washington: GPO, 1994), p. 471; U.S. Congress, Joint Committee on Printing, *1995-1996 Official Congressional Directory: 104th Congress*, 104th Cong., 1st sess., S.Pub. 104-14 (Washington: GPO, 1996), p. 417; U.S. Congress, Joint Committee on Printing, *1997-1998 Official Congressional Directory: 105th Congress*, 105th Cong., 1st sess., S.Pub. 105-20 (Washington: GPO, 1998), p. 439; U.S. Congress, Joint Committee on Printing, *1999-2000 Official Congressional Directory: 106th Congress*, 106th Cong., 1st sess., S.Pub. 106-21 (Washington: GPO, 2000), p. 423; U.S. Congress, Joint Committee on Printing, *2001-2002 Official Congressional Directory: 107th Congress*, 107th Cong., 1st sess., S.Pub. 107-20 (Washington: GPO, 2002), p. 430; U.S. Congress, Joint Committee on Printing, *2003-2004 Official Congressional Directory: 108th Congress*, 108th Cong., 1st sess., S.Pub. 108-18 (Washington: GPO, 2004), p. 425; U.S. Congress, Joint Committee on Printing, *2005-2006 Official Congressional Directory: 109th Congress*, 109th Cong., 1st sess., S.Pub. 109-12 (Washington: GPO, 2006), p. 434; U.S. Congress, Joint Committee on Printing, *2007-2008 Official Congressional Directory: 110th Congress*, 110th Cong., 1st sess., S.Pub. 110-13 (Washington: GPO, 2008), p. 432; U.S. Congress, Joint Committee on Printing, *2009-2010 Official Congressional Directory: 111th Congress*, 111th Cong., 1st sess., S.Pub. 111-14 (Washington: GPO, 2010), p. 444; H.Res. 6 and H.Res. 7 (113th Congress), agreed to January 3, 2013 ("Electing Members to Certain Standing Committees of the House of Representatives," *Congressional Record*, daily edition, vol. 159 (January 3, 2013), p. H23); and "Electing Members to Certain Standing Committees of the House of Representatives," *Congressional Record*, daily edition, vol. 159 (January 23, 2013), p. H250.

Notes:

a. Representative at Large (i.e., the state's only Member of the House of Representatives).

b. Appointed to replace Representative Chester G. Atkins.

c. Appointed to replace Representative Louis Stokes and Representative Gary L. Ackerman.

d. Most of the Members of the committee from the 104th Congress were appointed to the Select Committee on Ethics in the 105th Congress, which existed from January 7, 1997 to January 21, 1997. This select committee was established to resolve the Statement of Alleged Violations issued in the 104th Congress by the Committee on Standards of Official Conduct against the Speaker of the House. This select committee expired on January 21, 1997, with the House approving a reprimand against Speaker Newt Gingrich.

e. Appointed to the Select Committee on Ethics to complete the investigation begun by the Committee of Standards of Official Conduct.

f. Representative McDermott was briefly replaced (July 23 to July 24, 1996) by Representative Louis Stokes (D-OH) during a committee inquiry involving Representative McDermott.

g. Representative Berman was appointed as ranking member after Representative Mollohan's resignation.

h. Representative Tubbs-Jones died on August 20, 2008. Representative Gene Green served as acting chair for the remainder of the 110th Congress.

i. Representative Lofgren resigned as ranking member on January 26, 2011 ["Resignation as a Member of the Committee on Ethics," *Congressional Record*, daily edition, vol. 157 (January 26, 2011), p. H499].

j. Representative Hirono resigned from the committee on July 14, 2011 ["Resignation as Member of Committee on Ethics," *Congressional Record*, daily edition, vol. 157 (July 14, 2011), p. H5050].

k. Resident Commissioner Pierluisi represents the Commonwealth of Puerto Rico in the House and is the first Ethics Committee member who represents a territory. For more information on the Resident Commissioner, see CRS Report RL31856, *Resident Commissioner from Puerto Rico*, by R. Eric Petersen.

l. Representative Courtney was appointed to the committee on July 14, 2011 ["Electing a Member to a Certain Standing Committee of the House of Representatives," *Congressional Record*, daily edition, vol. 157 (July 14, 2011), p. H5050].

Author Contact Information

Jacob R. Straus
Analyst on the Congress
jstraus@crs.loc.gov, 7-6438